REFLECTIONS BESIDE STILL WATERS

EMBRACING EVERYDAY POSSIBILITIES
FOR GOODNESS, KINDNESS, AND PEACE

Steven J. Eiseman

Photographs: Judith Salstone

Fulton Books, Inc.
Meadville, PA

Published by Fulton Books 2020

ISBN 978-1-64654-301-4 (paperback)
ISBN 978-1-64654-348-9 (hardcover)
ISBN 978-1-64654-302-1 (digital)

Printed in the United States of America

To Maddie, Charlie, and Eva

My inspiration for wanting to share everything
true and beautiful I have learned along the way

He leadeth me beside the still waters.
He restoreth my soul.
—Psalm 23

Contents

Foreword

Lᴀᴛᴇ ɪɴ ᴛʜᴇ sᴜᴍᴍᴇʀ of 2002, as I struggled to adjust to life without my beloved mom, my father and I began attending Friday night Shabbat services at North Shore Congregation Israel in Glencoe, Illinois. We both found the experience comforting and healing. The liturgy was warm and life-affirming, the music beautiful, and a sense of peace always lingered long after the final prayers. When weather permitted, services were outside, overlooking a green expanse of lawn and trees, with Lake Michigan glinting in the day's fading light.

During one such service, Rabbi Lisa Greene devoted a sermon to the wisdom of preparing what she called an ethical will. She began her remarks by summarizing all the reasons virtually everyone at some point draws up a traditional will—the reassurance of directing one's own care and final arrangements, the joy of continuing to bless those we love, and the peace of knowing that the material things we have valued during our lifetimes will now enrich the lives of others.

Rabbi Greene then posed a gentle, spiritual challenge: Isn't it just as important to create and bequeath to those we love a clear statement of the essential wisdom we feel we've acquired over our lifetimes? Don't the values and ideals at the heart of our lives deserve thoughtful discussion and preservation? She spent the remainder of her sermon discussing the content of an ethical will and the opportunity it offers for sharing whatever kernels of truth and insight we may have discovered along the way.

In the years since that sermon, I have returned often to the concept of an ethical will, each time appreciating more strongly its value and benefits. I'm retired now, and at a point where I hope my learning and reading and thinking and living have produced a few conclusions worth sharing. What follows is a summary of those conclusions, interspersed liberally with quotations, references, and anecdotes that I hope add meaning and context.

And then there are those amazing photographs by Judith Salstone! Somewhere around my third rewrite, it dawned on me how beautifully the right pictures might complement and enhance the ideas I was exploring. I mentioned this possibility to my brother Robbie during one of our frequent Sunday afternoon walks through the parks of Evanston, and he immediately directed me to Judith's website.

What I found were photographs that were not only strikingly beautiful but also peaceful, meditative, and even nourishing in their effect on me. I contacted Judith, who is as generous with her time as she is with her talent. Within minutes, we had agreed on a joint project to blend pictures and words into an experience we hoped would be both affirming and uplifting.

So what started out as the framework for an ethical will has grown into a richer, more vivid discussion of values that Judith and I hope will be engaging philosophically, practically, and visually. The starting point of each short chapter is a photograph selected by Judith and a statement of one of the essential things I believe—signposts that keep me pointed in the direction I like to think I'm going.

I wouldn't characterize any of the writing that follows as particularly profound. I'm not even sure how much of my thinking is original. These are simply ideas that have stood up well for me over the years, ideas I continue to find nourishing and comforting. I offer them in the hope that some of what has enriched my life will be of value to others. What better reason is there for writing a will or, for that matter, any message from the heart?

SE

The Grace of Simple Goodness

And the Lord looked upon his creation and said it was good.
—Genesis 1:10

Nature does not demand that we be perfect. It requires only that we grow.
—Josh Liebman

The purpose of life is to contribute in some way to making things better.
—Robert F. Kennedy

I HAD FUN RECENTLY PUTTING together an anthology of my all-time favorite quotations in a piece I entitled *You Can Say That Again!* I devoted an entire chapter in the collection to passages from the Old and New Testaments that have always challenged and inspired me. One of those passages is the simple, iconic pronouncement in Genesis that begins this chapter.

I have thought a good deal over the years about the choice of the word *good* to describe God's handiwork. Theologically speaking, the Lord had just completed work on the entire cosmos—every galaxy, planet, and creature—and *good* is the word selected to describe God's self-assessment? One would certainly think any number of grander adjectives—such as *magnificent*, *glorious*, or even *perfect*—might have come closer to the mark. Most mornings when I pull back the drapes over the windows of my Lincoln Park apartment and gaze out appreciatively at Lake Michigan, I run out of words to describe its beauty. So why does the Bible settle on *good*?

I have no authoritative answer, of course, but the explanation I have come to embrace over the years is that there is an important message here, one of the first the Bible offers. Good is a worthwhile goal, even a holy one. In everything we undertake or pursue or accomplish over the course of our lives, if the results rise to the level of good, we have done something significant, something of which we can be proud. We have added a grain to the great storehouse of humanity's works, which began with man's arrival on the universal stage and will continue (we certainly hope!) for millennia to come.

This isn't to say we shouldn't strive for excellence—a consistent, exceptionally high level of practice or performance—in whatever parts of our lives we choose. And certainly mankind makes its most notable strides when remarkable individuals in every field of endeavor habitually insist on excellence. Nonetheless, Genesis's establishment of good as an eternal benchmark should remind us that you can't get to excellent without first achieving good.

This principle is nowhere more evident than in the world of sports. George Will once observed, "Sports serve society by providing vivid examples of excellence." As a lifelong Chicago Cubs fan, I confess that until recently I hadn't witnessed nearly as much excellence on the baseball diamond as I might have wished. (The Cubs' 2016 World Series championship wiped away a lifetime's worth of heartbreak in one glorious season!) But looking back, my years at Wrigley Field have afforded me more than a few examples of excellence and even an occasional glimpse of greatness.

Hall of Fame second baseman Ryne Sandberg is my favorite example. He was one of the finest players I've ever had the pleasure of watching. Over the course of his career, Sandberg's jaw-dropping, great plays made for a highlight reel that would be the envy of most major leaguers. But it was his amazing consistency in making the *routine* plays—the smooth pickups of ground balls, the hard and accurate throws to first, the fluid pivots and relays on double plays—that made him so invaluable day in and day out. It was Sandberg's dedication to being good—consistently, reliably, sometimes even boringly good—that helped him achieve the mantle of greatness.

It's the same in every profession and in every important part of our lives. We may never achieve greatness; few do. This is intrinsically true if you think of greatness, as I do, as achievement or creation of such a profound nature that it changes how the world perceives what is possible. But we can certainly be good at any number of the things we do. Being good is a decision, one we can make as often as we wish. It requires only that

we decide what is important to us, learn the skills we need, practice those skills, and do them repeatedly and conscientiously, without cutting corners.

James Bennis put it this way: "Don't just learn the tricks of the trade. Learn the trade!"

Good Is a Cornerstone of the Community

The older I get, the more deeply I appreciate how the small measure of good I manage to accomplish is completely dependent on the good work and service of those around me. There are some things I can do quite well for myself. Others I can manage with some level of competency. But I admit to a feeling of complete hopelessness when faced with a vast array of important tasks. My technical aptitude, for example, begins with hanging a picture reasonably straight and ends with attaching a document to an email.

The inescapable truth is that my happiness and security hinge on an enormous community of people around me willing to share their skills and fill in the ever-widening gap between what I need and what I can do for myself. No matter how self-sufficient most of us like to think of ourselves, ultimately we are all in the same boat. Each of us doing what we do well—with conscience and consistency—and counting on others to do the same is at the heart of the social contract on which we all base our lives. It is a fundamental way each of us enhances and enriches the lives of those around us.

Greatness is a marvel every time we are fortunate enough to witness it. And excellence is an admirable goal for many worthwhile endeavors. But striving for and achieving good—in any part of our lives—stands on its own as a blessing. Accomplishing something we and others can acknowledge as good should provide its own sense of satisfaction. It was, after all, the measuring stick for the very first act of creation and has remained so for every creative impulse ever since.

A Good Life is, at Heart, a Kind Life

Thou shalt love thy neighbor as thyself.
—Leviticus 19:18

For I was hungry and you gave me meat: I was thirsty, and you gave me drink: I was a stranger, and you took me in... Inasmuch as you have done it unto one of the least of these my brethren, you have done it unto me.
—Matthew 25:35–40

Let no one come to you without leaving better and happier. Be the living expression of God's kindness—kindness in your face, kindness in your eyes, kindness in your smile, kindness in your warm greeting.
—Mother Teresa

THE IMMEDIATE NATURAL COROLLARY of *achieving good* in the main endeavors of our lives is *doing good* throughout our lives. Scratch the surface of any good life, and you will find a foundation of kindness. Every major religion places a premium on acts of kindness, charity, and love. My understanding of Judaism's message in this regard is that *mitzvahs* (acts of goodness or kindness specifically blessed by God) are to be performed not for any thought of reward in this life or the hereafter but for the sheer joy of doing them *now*. I've never known it to fail. The moment you do something kind for others—willingly and wholeheartedly—your own life becomes, at least for that moment, richer and fuller.

There are a number of universally regarded virtues, and it is not my purpose here to discuss them all, much less rank them in importance. Honesty tops many lists of valued traits, and certainly honesty is a crucial part of every healthy relationship. Courage, faith, humility, and patience all have their advocates. But none of them holds a candle to kindness for the warmth and light it generates, the healing it promotes, and the hope it nourishes.

The ripples from a single act of kindness can expand and extend from one person to another, taking on a life of their own and potentially enriching an entire community, perhaps even the world. Hundreds of transformative endeavors (the Peace Corps, CARE, Special Olympics, Make-A-Wish Foundation, and Doctors Without Borders immediately come to mind) all began with a single, kind impulse that ultimately inspired and resonated around the world.

My brother Robbie spent several months living in Israel following his graduation from the University of Colorado in 1982. One of his favorite stories from that unforgettable period of his life occurred when he was on his way to Shabbat services in Jerusalem one Friday evening. A homeless man approached him on the street near the synagogue and asked him for whatever change he could spare.

When Robbie gave him what he had in his pocket, the man leveled a fixed stare at him and asked, "Aren't you forgetting something?" When Robbie responded that he couldn't think of anything, the man said, "You should thank me for giving you the opportunity to do a mitzvah!"

I love this story. Besides being a textbook example of *chutzpah* (unmitigated nerve!), this homeless man was hinting at a universal truth: an act of kindness—any kindness—benefits not only the recipient but also the person who performs the selfless act. The practice of kindness by even a few ennobles the entire community. In Genesis, God agreed to spare all of Sodom and Gomorrah if Abraham could find even ten righteous men there.

Kindness is potentially much more than a category of admirable behaviors. It can be a guiding philosophy for engaging the world and virtually everyone around us. In his biography of Saint Francis of Assisi, E. G. Chesterton relates a story I've always found inspiring. As Saint Francis wandered through thirteenth-century Italy, teaching and offering hope through his simple faith in God's goodness, he encountered people from every part of the social spectrum, from the most exalted royalty to the most desperate poverty. According to the account, every time Saint Francis met someone new, his reaction was the same; he was overcome with wonder and joy at the gift of experiencing yet one more wondrous manifestation of God's spirit.

I often think about what it would mean to live as Saint Francis lived. Imagine treating every human being you met as though he/she were, like you, a unique vessel of God's spirit, deserving not only your respect but also your veneration and love. Imagine a world where everyone treated one another that way. We might gain at least a glimmer of understanding into what it means to be made in God's image.

Unfortunately, I have to confess that although I believe completely in the truth of Saint Francis's vision, I find it next to impossible to act on it always. On far too many days, I allow whatever irritation, frustration, or disappointment I may be experiencing to dictate my response to those I encounter. I find myself identifying with my favorite *Peanuts* character, Linus, who once remarked in frustration, "I love mankind. It's *people* I can't stand!"

Small Acts and Simple Gestures

Despite my admitted failings (and those of all but the most enlightened among us), I believe it is possible to be a generally kind person and to approach others with a sense of warmth and acceptance. Kindness does not require saintliness. It requires only that we really look into the faces of those we encounter each day, engage them with a smile, and project the sense that they matter.

It starts with simple eye contact—looking up at someone you meet on the street or in an elevator or at a store rather than averting your gaze. In my experience, saying hello is an option with little downside. Even the briefest of pleasantries can connect you to another person in a way that subtly nourishes you both.

It requires very little effort to practice the small kindnesses that seem to be disappearing from our social landscape: being polite, holding the door for the person behind you, offering your seat on a bus to someone struggling, or slowing down on the highway to give another driver the space to merge. And as basic as it seems, saying "Thank you" for another's courtesy matters, often more than we may realize.

When I have a positive experience with any salesperson or service professional, I find that telling them I appreciate their work can be as important and meaningful as a generous tip. And if a restaurant server didn't do everything as well as I might have liked, a thank-you and a decent tip acknowledge that he/she still contributed to the enjoyment of my dining experience.

Is there ever *any* excuse for littering? People who throw garbage on the street or toss it out the car window are flipping off the entire world, saying in one careless, thoughtless gesture that no one matters except them. Organizations and countries that pollute the atmosphere, strip mine mountaintops, clear cut forests, and pour waste into rivers and oceans are just taking littering to its irrevocable, hideous extreme. Conservation always comes down to individual action—each of us resolving not to add even one more wrapper or piece of plastic to this turquoise jewel of a world we all share. And there's no reason, every once in a while, we can't pick up someone else's litter and toss it away. What's the point of being our brother's keeper if we draw the line at slobs?

I can't imagine kindness without generosity. Being generous—with our time and attention, our talents and resources—is how we translate kindness into action. It's a crucial connection, because kindness without action is like a chocolate chip cookie without chocolate. It's still basically good, I suppose, but is capable of being *so* much better! Generosity is nothing more than a tendency to respond with whatever we have to offer to whoever comes into our lives, from those we love to those we may encounter once and never see again.

In my experience, it's the constant strain of daily demands in every part of our lives that poses the greatest challenge to a generous spirit. When our days are supercharged with stress, pressures, and expectations, it can feel as though we're doing all we can just to remain civil. Kindness may seem like a luxury, particularly when all we're trying to do is make it through the day.

Even so, taking a minute to do what we can for those in need standing right in front of us feels like a moral imperative to me. Otherwise, kindness becomes a matter of convenience, not conscience. For example, I have friends who make it a point never to give money to those who approach them on the street because "most of them are only going to use it to buy booze or drugs." My position is that it really doesn't make any difference how a person uses what we give him/her. We don't have any control over that anyway.

The point is that someone has asked us for a kindness. We have an opportunity to respond. When we do, we create a connection, however brief, with another soul. And it is these connections—born of kindness and compassion—that strengthen the fabric of humanity.

Happiness Starts with a Sense of Wonder and Gratefulness

O Lord, how manifold are thy works! In wisdom hast thou made them all: the earth is full of thy riches.
—Psalm 104:24

Never once in my life did I ask God for success or wisdom or power or fame. I asked for wonder, and He gave it to me.
—Abraham Joshua Heschel

When a person doesn't have gratitude, something is missing in his or her humanity.
—Elie Wiesel

APPRECIATING AND VALUING THE life each of us has been given is the beginning of a reverence for all life. It is also the beginning of happiness, which I would characterize as a general sense of well-being, contentment, and peace. I believe that happiness can be an intrinsic part of the human experience, as fundamental as birth, growth, learning, striving, pain, loss, and love. It may at times be absent from our lives, perhaps even for prolonged periods, but it is never irrevocably lost to us. The possibility of happiness in our lives continues until we take our final breath.

Certainly the possibility of happiness is not the same thing as a promise or guarantee. Benjamin Franklin pointed out that the Declaration of Independence speaks only of our right to the *pursuit* of happiness. He added wisely, "You have to catch up with it yourself."

It makes sense to me to distinguish happiness from such other experiences as joy, ecstasy, or bliss. These emotional states, while wonderful, are also fleeting, unsustainable, and rare enough for most of us that we don't bank on them, like winning a lottery. By contrast, happiness is something with which virtually all of us have had some experience. And although no one can be happy all the time, the possibility of happiness helps sustain us throughout our lives, even during the darkest times.

I think it's safe to say that we all crave happiness and that most of us are convinced we don't experience it nearly as often as we would like. It's tempting to think of happiness as having certain ironclad prerequisites—i.e., to be happy, we must have good health, freedom from pain, financial security, rewarding work, a few luxuries, love, and companionship.

But it's also certain that most of us have gone through periods when we have lacked the majority of these things and still held on to some measure of happiness. Additionally, we may be fortunate enough to have witnessed the courageous spirit of individuals who must deal daily with catastrophic illness, tragic loss, or crushing poverty—things difficult for many of us even to imagine—and still maintain a sense of purpose and optimism. These remarkable folks undoubtedly have periods of terrible sadness and even despair. But rather than be crushed, as many in their circumstances undoubtedly are, they somehow find room in their lives for perseverance, faith, and hope.

The Recipe's a Mystery, but Not the Ingredients

I don't pretend to have any definite answer to how it is that happiness blossoms perennially in some hearts while so rarely taking root in others. But I would venture that if there is one thing that all happiness-inclined people share, it is a sense of wonder and gratefulness: wonder at the grandeur, beauty, and mystery all around them and gratefulness for the simple, good things in their lives.

Gratefulness starts the moment we begin paying attention, thoughtfully and deliberately, to the many things in our lives that nourish us. My favorite scene in Woody Allen's film *Manhattan* occurs near the end of the story, when the main character asks rhetorically why one should want to go on living in a chaotic, violent universe with no purpose or hope. He decides the answer is simple. There are certain things that make life worth living. For him, those things include Frank Sinatra, Groucho Marx, autumn in Central Park, and the face of the young woman he suddenly realizes he loves most of all.

The reason I find this scene both touching and relevant to our discussion is that I believe we all have lists like that—treasured assortments of people, places, pleasures, and experiences that we love and that make our lives sweet. My list, for example, would start with spending time with my nieces and nephew and go on to include fresh strawberries, dark chocolate, Mark Twain, the Chicago Cubs, Nat King Cole, all four seasons, *The Catcher in the Rye*, Beethoven's Sixth Symphony, Vincent Van Gogh, and the view of Lake Michigan from my balcony. I'd also throw in Van Morrison's "Bright Side of the Road." I defy anyone to listen to that song and not feel at least a little happier!

It's tempting not to give much thought to these glimmers of light and beauty that ripple through our lives. Certainly we recognize them and appreciate their value whenever we experience them. But I would suggest that one of the keys to happiness is being mindful—continually, peacefully aware—of whom and what we love, even when our attention and efforts are focused elsewhere. The result can be an ever-deepening joy in our blessings and the realization that gratefulness and happiness are so closely connected that one is never present without the other.

Steps in the Right Direction

Although no two people are likely to define happiness in quite the same way, I submit there are two simple actions that increase the possibility of happiness, no matter how we define it. The first involves doing something kind or generous for someone else. I find it doesn't matter who that someone is or what specifically we do, as long as we do it wholeheartedly and without expecting anything in return. Ralph Waldo Emerson once observed, "It is one of the most beautiful compensations of this life that no man can sincerely try to help another without helping himself." He's right. The simple act of doing something good for others contributes, inevitably and wonderfully, to feeling good about ourselves.

Second, we can do something every day to appreciate and enjoy the beauty of the world. When burdens and hardship leave us feeling overwhelmed, just getting outside for a few minutes can calm body and spirit. I find it helps to take deep, slow breaths and let my mind wander. Or take a moment to stretch. Or go for a short walk. If a walk isn't possible, opening a window or just gazing outside for a while creates a little breathing space. Daydream. Look at a favorite picture of something beautiful or someone you love. If you are not feeling happy, I promise you will at least feel better.

The Importance of Balance, Abundance of Love, and Comfort of Prayer

Let the words of my mouth, and the meditation of my heart, be acceptable in thy sight, O Lord, my strength and my redeemer.
　　　　　　　　　　—Psalm, 19:14

Live a balanced life. Learn some and think some and play and work some every day.
　　　　　　　　　　—Robert Fulghum

I pray because I can't help myself. Because the need pours out of me all the time, waking and sleeping. It doesn't change God, it changes me.
—William Nicholson, *Shadowlands*

THERE'S A TOUCHING MOMENT in the movie *The Karate Kid*, in which the wise karate master, Mr. Miyagi, reminds his student, Daniel Larusso, "Daniel-san, you remember lesson about balance? Lesson not just karate only. Lesson for whole life."

Creating space in the heart for happiness to flourish requires a balance among competing needs and responsibilities that often feels impossible to attain. Love, work, friendship, family—all the things that nourish the spirit and make us whole—require time and attention. There never seems to be enough of either for any of us to feel we are caring sufficiently for everyone and everything precious to us. We do the best we can.

Often the first casualty in the nonstop juggling act of our daily lives is *ourselves*. Finding time and space for ourselves while meeting our many obligations to others is crucial. And so much depends on it. I believe the only way we can continue to give healthily and happily to others is by constantly replenishing ourselves. Otherwise, we are likely to find we have less and less to offer those who count on us.

Taking care of ourselves demands taking time to do the things that keep us healthy, nourished, and strong. This is much easier said than done, and I confess I have never been very good at it. For most of my life, I found it easier to focus my energy, care, and concern on those around me. I told myself that my own needs were at best a secondary concern and, at worst, a guilty self-indulgence.

I chose a career at the Juvenile Court of Cook County that I loved, and that pretty well guaranteed there would be an unending procession of troubled children and families vying for my attention and involvement. It was easy to pretend my own needs were far less important than those of clients and others in my life and that there was no cost to postponing the time, relaxation, and care I too seldom allowed myself.

The consequences of this delusion caught up with me during the final years of my career. For over three decades, my workplace had felt like a second home to me. Suddenly, I found that most mornings, I was tired by the time I finished the short walk from my car to the court building. And the weariness never really lifted; it continued throughout the day. It took me a while to understand my quandary. I was certain my idealism and commitment were as deep as ever. I just came to realize that my resilience—my ability to adjust to change, handle pressure, and avoid feeling overwhelmed—was not. I felt like a well that was close to running dry.

I don't believe there is any formula for achieving balance that will work for everyone. All I can offer here is a conviction that each one of us has a right to a few precious minutes during the course of each day that we reserve just for ourselves. Examples that have become increasingly important to me include taking multiple short breaks during the work day, allowing time for a leisurely lunch, keeping weekends mostly work-free, taking *every single* vacation day, and getting in some exercise a few times each week. When enjoying a favorite food or beverage (alcoholic or otherwise!), there's nothing wrong with indulging ourselves once in a while.

My point is that whatever activities, pastimes, or simple satisfactions relax us and help us feel good, we need to do them—regularly and often. They multiply our moments of happiness, which in turn allow us to be greater channels of happiness into the lives of others.

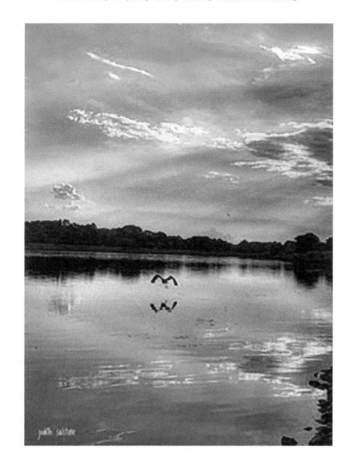

Opportunities for Love Abound—We Benefit Every Time We Say Yes!

Each day presents a fresh opportunity to talk and *listen* to those we love. Psychiatrist M. Scott Peck states in *The Road Less Traveled*, "The principal form that the work of love takes is attention. When we love another, we give him or her our attention.… By far the most common and important way in which we can exercise our attention is by listening."

When we think about those to whom we make it a point to listen and devote our attention, it's natural for an intimate partner or romantic interest to come first to mind. Walk into any library or bookstore and you'll find entire sections devoted to the topic of romantic love—how to find it, nourish it, strengthen and sustain it. The sheer number of new titles every year suggests a great many of us live in constant hope that someone out there can help us figure it all out.

The self-help industry can relax! I won't be competing for space on their bookshelves anytime soon. As a single man in his sixties who continues to struggle with love's multiple challenges, I have never been able to find sustained fulfillment in this important part of my life. And I really don't think I'm any closer to answers now than I was in my thirties. About the only wisdom I've gained is that I no longer try to analyze other people's relationships or sift through them for clues that might help me understand why they're working. If someone I care for is happy with the love he/she has found, that's good enough for me.

I am thrilled and awed by couples I know who have found deep, sustained happiness together, undoubtedly far greater than any they would have known separately. But I also realize that what these fortunate folks have worked so hard to create is uniquely their own, unlikely to be something I can either replicate or adopt as a blueprint for myself.

I'm not suggesting that when it comes to love, we can't learn from the examples of others. Virtually everyone agrees that developing certain skills (e.g., listening, affirming, nurturing, problem-solving) improves our chances for long-term romantic success. It's just that when relationships are going well, all the skills we've acquired and lessons we've learned don't fully explain our good fortune. And when love goes south, after we finish obsessing over all the possible reasons, we often find we're no closer to understanding what happened: when and why someone we once cherished began mattering less to us or stopped caring so much about us.

In my case, although experience and plenty of soul searching and therapy have led me to believe singlehood may make the most sense for me, I'm still leaving the relationship door open a crack. I miss the love and deep connection that for many years have been missing from my life. At the same time, I remain convinced that my (or anyone's) faltering pursuit of intimacy in no way limits the possibility of love springing up anywhere and anytime and in deeply satisfying ways that may have nothing to do with romance.

The ebb and flow of love throughout my life has left me at least one bit of insight: A satisfying love life is not a prerequisite for leading a life filled with love. The net of love that each of us casts out into the world doesn't necessarily begin or end with our lovers, spouses, or children. It can cover so many more, if we let it. Family, friends, neighbors, colleagues, clients, kids (our own and/or others'), teachers, mentors, students, kindred spirits of any age, and even pets can fill our lives and overflow our hearts. I think often of the lifelong procession of unforgettable souls, relatively few of them romantic partners, who have found their way into my heart and never left. They have been my gateway to peaks of joy—and sometimes depths of vulnerability, need, and pain—more powerful and overwhelming than any I ever thought I could experience.

Even when those emotions have lain comfortably dormant for years, they come roaring back to life every time my feelings for someone begin to deepen and grow. In those moments, I wonder if the question we all face is not whether to allow love into our lives (it often finds a way in, whether we allow it or not) but whether to hold fast to love, even when it steers us toward uncharted waters. Are we willing for love to move us out of our comfort and complacency and perhaps lead us to feel differently about parts of our lives we thought we had settled, figured out, or decided? I'm not always sure that I am. But I like to think I'm at least open to the possibility.

A Word Here about Prayer

Prayer is as deeply personal and profound an expression of one's spirit as any of us may ever make. Every religion offers an abundance of prescribed prayers to help its adherents open their hearts to God. These are often quite beautiful declarations of love and faith and unquestionably useful as a starting point for a lifelong relationship to God.

But liturgy is just that—a starting point. Prayer can and should be much more than that. Each of us is free to communicate with God however and whenever we wish, in words and ways that are uniquely our own. We can convey whatever is in our hearts, whatever hopes we cherish for ourselves, for our loved ones and for all mankind. Most of all, we can express simple gratitude for the blessings that fill our lives.

I'd like to make one suggestion here: Begin each day with a simple prayer, giving thanks for the gift of the new day. Use whatever words you like. Pray for or about anything else you wish. Just be mindful for a moment of what you've been given and all that you now have the freedom to do. I think you'll find it will be worth it.

Friendship and Laughter: Making the Journey a Joy

If I am not for myself, who am I? If I am not for others, what am I? If not now, when?
—Rabbi Hillel

Every gift from a friend is a wish for your happiness.
—Richard Bach

Laughter is not a bad beginning for a friendship, and it is by far the best ending.
—Oscar Wilde

FRIENDSHIP IS ONE OF life's greatest blessings. Friends contribute immeasurably to our sense of security, value, fulfillment, and peace. They lift our spirits, lighten our burden, and allow us the grace of feeling that we're not alone. I would argue the benefits of friendship are far more qualitative than quantitative; one can surely gain as much from one or two good friends as from multiple friends.

And friends make us laugh! As unique as each of my friends is, they all get me laughing—often uncontrollably and always healingly. They also get me thinking and feeling and caring and loving. Friendship stretches our humanity and our capacity for love. In his wise little book *Illusions*, Richard Bach writes, "Family is not so much a matter of blood, as it is a matter of love and regard for another human soul. Members of one's true family rarely grow up under the same roof." Nurturing and rejoicing in our family—those to whom we are bound spiritually as well as biologically—enrich every other facet of our lives.

Nothing promotes happiness like laughter. It's hard to imagine one without the other. In his popular account of his own recovery from catastrophic illness, *Anatomy of an Illness*, Norman Cousins writes extensively of the connection between laughter and general health and well-being. He cites research on endorphins, the body's own natural painkillers, which course through the body during laughter. He points to laughter's salutary effects on respiration, heart rate, and circulation. Part of his own self-prescription for managing his care and recovery was to watch his favorite movie comedies for hours each day and to surround himself with friends he loved and with whom he loved to laugh.

Cousins' results are not scientific, and the health benefits he feels he achieved through his methods are clearly anecdotal. Nonetheless, it would be hard for even the most empirical of medical researchers to argue against the relationship between happiness and wellness. And although there are undoubtedly many paths to happiness, I contend that virtually all of them include friendship and laughter.

Experiencing the Infinite in the Everyday

And God said, Let us make man in our image, after our likeness.
—Genesis 1:26

The whole idea of compassion is based on a keen awareness of the interdependence of all living beings, which are all part of one another, and all involved in one another.
—Thomas Merton

There are only two ways to live your life. One is as though nothing is a miracle. The other is as though everything is a miracle.
—Albert Einstein

I BELIEVE EVERYONE HAS A spiritual life, just as everyone has a physical life and an emotional life. This is true, regardless of one's religion or culture, and certainly includes agnostics and atheists. After all, faith is reflected as much in what we do, as it is in how (or even whether) we worship. I don't think it matters at all whether we invoke God by name or what name we choose to give God's presence in our lives. What matters is opening ourselves to wonder and awe and mystery and embracing a sense of gratefulness for life's gifts.

Just as we choose whether to take care of our bodies or take them for granted, so do we decide whether to nourish our spirits or ignore them. It's my strong conviction that nourishing the spirit makes us far more receptive to happiness and far more likely to be a source of happiness for others.

This brings me to the passage from Genesis that begins this section—the creation of man in God's image. It is the biblical verse I find most inspiring while, at the same time, virtually impossible to comprehend. I love to think of myself and all those with whom I share this world as created in God's image. It's uplifting to think of ourselves and our hopes of adding a measure of goodness and love to the world as somehow a reflection of God's will.

Yet isn't it the height of presumption to believe that *any* of us has any absolute insight to God's nature or will? Comic writer Jane Wagner once asked, "What is reality, really, but a collective hunch?" She's right, of course, and having conceded the truth of that humorous observation about physical reality, how infinitely more beyond our understanding must God be.

Every major religious tradition teaches that God is infinite and transcendent. This is a fundamental part of most cultures' understanding of the Eternal. Yet so many well-meaning people of faith—religious leaders and followers alike—have a tendency to speak with absolute, unshakable certainty about God's wishes and intentions, as though they have the Eternal on speed dial.

These kinds of pronouncements, even when uttered by inspirational, devout individuals, always strike me as arrogant and slightly ridiculous. If God inhabits the realm of the eternal, as we all seem to agree, then doesn't it follow that the Lord's will must be, finally and unequivocally, beyond the minuscule limits of our human understanding? The infinite, by definition, is impossible for any of us to comprehend, much less describe. This doesn't mean that we give up on trying to live in accordance with the moral/religious principles we cherish or that we stop listening to those much wiser than we in spiritual matters. It does mean that when it comes to the holy and the eternal, we're all on the same journey and we should proceed with open hearts and deep humility.

It seems to me that no matter how lofty our intelligence or profound our faith, any knowledge of God we think we have must always remain tiny and tentative. Yet I would suggest that there are those rare moments when it is possible to sense God's presence. Aren't we aware of something beyond ourselves when our hearts overflow with love or when we experience beauty that overwhelms our senses? Isn't there something eternal in those moments when joy fills us so utterly that all we can do is remain simply, quietly grateful or when we suddenly know with unexplainable certainty that there is something that knits the entire universe together and connects us to everyone and everything else?

For me this is the nearness of God. There are certainly other ways to speak of such glimmers of awe. Some settle on terms like *perfection*, *wonderment*, or *magic* to characterize what they've experienced. In every case, I believe we're all just trying to express the inexpressible—to convey something that eclipses our senses and has led us to an awareness beyond our capacity to describe or share.

Every religion prescribes its own unique approach to God, and each evokes beauty and wonder. I have always found the Jewish tradition beautiful and fulfilling. However, since God is infinite, it stands to reason that there must be infinite paths to God's presence. Each of us is free to choose his/her own path or to experience many different ones during our lives. Regardless of the paths we choose, if the journey deepens our understanding of what is good and beautiful and true, an awareness of God will blossom, gradually but surely, in our hearts.

Some Final Thoughts and Acknowledgments

How good it is, and how pleasant, when all men dwell together as one.
—Psalm 133

We have what we seek. It is there all the time, and if we give it time, it will make itself known to us.
—Thomas Merton

Do the best you can, and don't take life too serious.
—Will Rogers

As I REREAD THESE pages, it's pretty clear that nothing they contain is even remotely revelatory or complicated. That's fine. It's been my experience that simple truths are often the most important anyway. At the very least, I hope I've kept it simple: value the good you and others do, prioritize kindness, strive for balance, be grateful for everyone and everything that sustain you, open yourself to the wonder and holiness in your life.

I'd be the first to admit that all this is much easier said than done. It's hard to avoid getting caught up in the turmoil, stress, and anger that swirl all around us, and we can be forgiven if at times we succumb to the negativity and even add to it. It's often tempting to label people and write them off for their politics or worldview. But each of us also has the ability to calm things down, regain our moral footing, and exercise a little patience and tolerance. We can at least try to see others' points of view. And each of us can contribute a little healing and forgiveness and grace to the world.

So much of the grace I have enjoyed throughout my life flows from family and friends, many of whom encouraged me not only to write these reflections but also to share them. When my father, Leonard Eiseman, finished reading my first draft during the final months of his life, his first comment was, "You really should put this out there. A lot of people think about these things, and they might appreciate your take on them." My sister and brother, Cathy Nemeth and Rob Eiseman, were my sounding board for every idea and theme and gave me the confidence to sit down and just start writing.

My lifelong friends Bruce Koff, Brad Falkof, Genie Kahn, and Dr. Bob Elson all touched me with the warmth of their reactions and insistence that maybe this one shouldn't just sit on a shelf, like so many of my other retirement projects. And special thanks to my friend Dr. Jill Ostrow, who more than anyone else helped me shape this little book into something I hope will offer others an occasional moment of clarity and comfort.

One of my own constant comforts is the psalm that begins this section. Its message reminds me that more unites us than divides us—always. We are all doing the best we can to find a measure of sanity and peace. And we all deserve the benefit of the doubt.

Our search for happiness and fulfillment continues throughout our lives. The answers we find are never perfect and rarely permanent. But it seems to me they all should lead us to sharpen our focus on the things that are most important to us and to rejoice in those we love. That's as good a place to start as any. And in the words of Dan Millman, "Stop trying to figure everything out. You don't have to understand the ocean to swim in it." To that I would add, whatever you do manage to figure out, pass it on!

SE

About the Authors

Steven J. Eiseman recently retired from the Juvenile Court of Cook County in Chicago, where he devoted thirty-two years to providing care, guidance, and opportunity to struggling children and families. His relationships with many of these children have extended into their adulthood and continue to this day. The programs he designed and developed during his career continue to serve thousands of children every year and have been adopted by court systems across the country. Before coming to the Juvenile Court, Steve worked for several years for the Salvation Army, counseling and assisting adult offenders.

Steve holds a master's degree in management / human resource development from National Louis University and earned his undergraduate degree from Carleton College, majoring in government and international relations. He attended the University of Edinburgh in Scotland for a year, studying jurisprudence, literature, and oral tradition.

Steve lives in Chicago, not too far from Wrigley Field, where you can find him during every Cubs home stand. He is a movie and theater buff, a fan of the daily newspaper (the folding kind, *not* the online variety!), and a supporter of numerous social and environmental causes. His greatest joy is simply spending relaxed, unstructured time with friends and family, especially his beloved nieces and nephew. This book is dedicated to them.

*****

Judith Salstone has devoted much of the past six years to creating photographs that are both stunningly beautiful and deeply spiritual. Her canvas is the parks, lakes, and woods of Chicago and its northern suburbs, as well as the ever-changing moods and vistas of Lake Michigan. The profound sense of joy and wonder at the heart of Judith's work is something she embraces as a gift after years spent working to overcome challenges that threatened her health and her most cherished relationships.

Judith feels fortunate that she never has to look far for inspiration. She finds it every time she walks out her front door and encounters everyday patterns of light and color and sky and water, which suddenly become transformed when she views them from a slightly different angle or in a subtly different light. Her favorite shots capture simple natural scenes that for a brief instant shine with astonishing brilliance before becoming ordinary once again.

Judith is motivated by a constant sense of gratitude for her ever-deepening awareness of the beauty all around her and a passion for sharing that beauty with others. Photography allows her to do this and, in the process, ensures that the moments, images, and impressions she has captured are available to all who wish to experience them with her.

Judith's work is available for viewing on the following:

- Website: www.judithsalstone.com
- Facebook: Majestic Sunsets and Sunrises
- Instagram: @magesticsky

CPSIA information can be obtained
at www.ICGtesting.com
Printed in the USA
LVHW070359111120
671259LV00012B/291

9 781646 543483